Basketball History

Court Chronicles – The Evolution, Teams, and
Players That Shaped the Game

How to get $98 worth of Sports Cards Research for Free

Free Bonus #1 ($49 value)

"7 Things You Must Do Before Buying A Sports Card"

Free Bonus #2 ($49 value)

Our Custom Spreadsheet To Help You Visualize The Price Trending And Projections Of Your Favorite Sports Cards.

To get your Bonuses go to

https://betosalinas.activehosted.com/f/1

Table of Contents

INTRODUCTION 1

CHAPTER 1: MADNESS IN MASSACHUSETTS 3

    Duck on a Rock...3
    Peach Baskets and Soccer Balls 4
    Thirteen Rules...5
    Game Time 7

CHAPTER 2: PLAYING DIRTY 12

    Roughnecks...12
    Judging by the Court 14
    Stop the Spread 15
    Cagers..16
    Game Time 18

CHAPTER 3: NEXT LEVEL 22

    Expansion and Great Expectations 24
    Blackballed 25
    The Harlem Globetrotters and Their Contribution to Professional Basketball...27
    Color-Blind 29
    Game Time 30

CHAPTER 4: THE BALL'S IN YOUR COURT 34

    Gambling and the Evolution of College Basketball...................................34
    Television's Influence 37
    Dribbling for Dollars...39
    Game Time 43

CHAPTER 5: RIVALS 46

    From Auditoriums to Stadiums...46
    NBA—The Final Frontier..47
    Game Time 49

CHAPTER 6: WE ARE THE CHAMPIONS...53

    The Chosen Ones..53

WHAT MAKES A CHAMPIONSHIP TEAM? 54

TOP 10 CHAMPIONSHIP TEAMS OF ALL TIME 56

GAME TIME 60

CHAPTER 7: DYNASTY AND LEGACY **65**

NBA DYNASTIES PAST AND PRESENT 67

LEAVING IT ALL ON THE COURT 68

SMALL FORWARDS, BIG POWER..75

THE CHANGING OF THE GUARD...79

AT THE CENTER 85

GAME TIME 87

CONCLUSION **91**

GAME TIME ANSWER GUIDE **93**

REFERENCES...**98**

PHOTO CREDITS 105

Introduction

It's a frigid winter day in 1891 in Springfield, Massachusetts. The frost outside has kept a group of young adult male athletes inside for several days. Used to playing hard contact sports like rugby and football, these young men have been getting more and more restless by the day, and eventually start fighting in the hallways. Then, one day, the YMCA's physical education instructor, James Naismith, calls the athletes to the gymnasium. They grudgingly anticipate another boring child's game, like the ones they've been forced to play during the cold spell, and so report unenthusiastically.

Five minutes later, they are scrambling over each other, pummeling one another with bare fists and kicking other athletes in a free-for-all scrimmage to get a soccer ball to get in—and stay in—a wooden basket. After an hour or more, only one ball makes it and stays, ending the game. Thus began the sport of basketball.

Today, the basket has been replaced by a net and iron rims on a raised plexiglass backboard. Naismith's 13 rules, which he created to govern the sport after the brawl, have now become gigantic binders full of rules and regulations regarding everything from fouls to shoes, endorsement deals, and lifestyle.

In the early days, basketball players came from a group of mostly burly rugby and football players and other young men who played lacrosse. Today, bulk has been replaced by height, with 7-foot-tall icons like LeBron James who can throw a ball into a basket up to 84 feet away (Luke, 2021). The average basketball player is about 6 feet 7 inches tall and any player over 7 feet usually has no problem getting drafted into the National Basketball Association (NBA).

Tyrone "Muggsy" Bogues wasn't blessed with height. At 5 feet 3 inches tall, and the shortest man to ever play professional basketball, he played side by side with 7-foot-7 Manut Boll. Bogues proved that heart could win over height. Other players hated playing against Bogues, one of the most significant point guards ever drafted to the NBA. Some even tried to get him banned from the league, complaining that he was too short to play. His speed, agility, determination, and knowledge of the game and how to play it frustrated his opponents. Known for his incredible defensive skills, including his quickness and his ability to strip the ball from bigger, taller players, Bogues was a disruptor. In his career, he was credited with over 1,300 steals, and over 6,700 assists (Nonstop, 2020; Whistle, 2013). His low center of gravity proved to be the taller players' Achilles heel. His indefatigable heart and knowledge of how to play the game with finesse and power gave the opposing teams a metaphorical coronary. He was considered "the best overall defender in NBA history" (Goalcast, 2022).

Much more has changed since the advent of that first basketball game. Rules, dress codes, team size, marketing, management, and the idea of team ownership have all brought new ideologies and images to the game. The advent of television took the game to another level of national and international acclaim. Today's game is a far cry from Naismith's original design, but, without his creative genius, the game of basketball would never have existed at all.

By looking back at the most dominant players and teams in the game, throughout this book you'll be able to see how Naismith's original slow-moving idea became the fast-paced, world-renowned game that continues to impact the lives of boys and girls, men and women, all over the world today. Put your new knowledge of basketball trivia to the test at the end of each chapter. Make these questions part of your next game night. If you're a middle- or high-school basketball coach, use the *Game Time* trivia to inspire and educate your team.

Chapter 1:

Madness in Massachusetts

It's December 1891. A treacherous New England storm has kept several adolescent men cooped up inside their dormitories for days. Accustomed to the rigor of outdoor sports like rugby, soccer, and lacrosse, these young men are sick of methodical marching indoors, gymnastics, calisthenics, and children's games. Their boredom begins to manifest in bad tempers, roughhousing, and fights. How to keep these 30 to 40 restless souls from killing each other was the problem James Naismith, International Training School physical education teacher for the Springfield, Massachusetts YMCA, had to find an answer to—and quickly! The solution to this problem became what we know today as basketball.

Duck on a Rock

"Duck on a rock" was a medieval game played by Naismith and his childhood buddies. The rules were simple. A smaller rock was placed atop a large one. One child was assigned to guard the smaller rock as the other children threw stones in the hope of knocking it off the larger one. Once the rock was knocked off, the guard had to put it back in place before the others had gathered all their rocks. If he was able to do so, he could tag another child to be the guard. Not every child was a great shot, and you had to be pretty quick to get out of the way and retrieve the stone once it was knocked off.

From his youth, Naismith was an avid sportsman. He played rugby, football, soccer, and lacrosse, and was an experienced gymnast. He understood the importance of hand–eye coordination and the stamina, endurance, strength, passion, and fortitude it takes to excel in sports. When Naismith graduated from McGill University in 1888, he was awarded a gold medal for best all-around athlete. He knew the frustration the Springfield, Massachusetts boys were feeling in 1891 and, based on his athletic experiences, he came up with a brilliant idea.

Peach Baskets and Soccer Balls

Naismith's original idea was to use two boxes at opposite ends of the YMCA's indoor gymnasium, tacked below a rail 10 feet from the floor, with the goal of lobbing a soccer ball into the boxes. However, all the janitor could find were two tapered wooden baskets with slats that had been used to deliver peaches. Undaunted, Naismith grabbed the two baskets and nailed them to the walls.

When Naismith's students, whom he called to the gym, saw the two peach baskets, they didn't know what was going on. They probably thought it was just another kids' game. They were not enthusiastic.

Naismith explained his game and broke the boys up into two teams. The winning team would be the one that could get the ball in the basket and keep it there. He blew the whistle and the game began, but it wasn't the pleasant, easy-going fun he expected.

Used to running, pushing, shoving, throwing elbows, and tripping one another to score a goal, all of the boys "tackled, kicked, punched each other in a free-for-all that landed them in a heap on the gymnasium floor. When Naismith pulled them apart, there were several black eyes, bruises, a concussion, and dislocated shoulder" (Springfield College, 2015). Naismith realized he would need to get very clear on game rules if these young men were going to survive.

Thirteen Rules

The first basketball games moved slowly. On December 21, 1891, William Chase led the first nine-member team to victory after his 25-foot throw landed a soccer ball in the basket that actually stayed there. The final score in the hour-long game was 1–0 (Basketball.org. n.d.). By contrast, Stephen Curry, point guard for the Golden State Warriors, scored 30 points and completed six rebounds and two assists in 30 minutes in the first Warriors playoff game against the Sacramento Kings on April 15, 2023. De'Aaron Fox of the Kings scored 29 points and 5 assists in the second half of the game (NBA, 2023). Can you imagine the Los Angeles Lakers with no running game and no dribbling?

Students were posted in the balcony to retrieve balls that actually scored. However, they also impeded the teams' progress by slapping the ball away from the basket. A janitor was tasked with climbing a ladder to recover the ball too.

Teams consisted of a minimum of nine players but, in all later games, team size was dependent on the size of the playing field and the number of people in the class. According to Naismith's new rules, free throws were first considered a punishment but later became a part of the game. Guards were assigned to guard the basket and retrieve the ball. In all, there were 13 rules which were (Klein, 2022):

1. The ball can be thrown in any direction with one or both hands.

2. The ball may be batted in any direction with one or both hands, never with the fists.

3. Players can't use the arms or the body to hold the ball.

4. No shouldering, holding, pushing, tripping, or striking in any way the person of an opponent. First infringement counts as a

foul, second disqualifies a player until the next goal is made, or if there was evident intent to injure the person, for the whole game, no substitute allowed.

5. Hitting the ball with your fist is a foul.

6. If either side makes three consecutive fouls it shall count as a goal for the opponents (consecutive means without the opponents in the meantime making a foul).

7. A goal shall be made when the ball is thrown or batted from the grounds into the basket and stays there, providing those defending the goal do not touch or disturb the goal.

8. If the ball rests on the edges, and the opponent moves the basket, it shall count as a goal.

9. When the ball goes out of bounds it shall be thrown into the field of play by the person first touching it. In case of a dispute the umpire shall throw it straight into the field. The thrower-in is allowed 5 seconds; if he holds it longer it shall go to the opponent. If any side persists in delaying the game, the umpire shall call a foul on that team.

10. The umpire shall be the judge of the men and shall note the fouls and notify the referee when three consecutive fouls have been made. He shall have the power to disqualify men according to rule five.

11. The referee shall be the judge of the ball and shall decide when the ball is in play, in bounds, to which side it belongs, and shall keep the time. He shall decide when a goal has been made, and keep account of the goals, with any other duties that are usually performed by the referee.

12. The time shall be two 15-minute halves, with 5 minutes rest between.

13. The side making the most goals in that time shall be declared the winner. In case of a draw, the game may be by mutual agreement, be continued until another goal is made.

Game Time

How to Play

Divide your group into teams or play one-on-one with a friend. Answer all the *Game Time* questions from the text and your basketball knowledge for two points each. Test your basketball trivia knowledge by answering the bonus questions for three points each. Tally up your score at the end of each chapter.

1. Which of Naismith's 13 rules does not apply today?

    a. A player cannot run while holding the ball.

    b. The ball must be held in or between the hands. The arms or body must not be used for holding it.

    c. If either side makes three consecutive fouls, it shall count as a goal for the opponents.

2. Who was Naismith's star player in the first ever basketball game?

    a. Chase Williams

    b. William Smith

    c. William Chase

3. Who was the shortest man ever to play professional basketball for the NBA?

    a. Monte Towe

    b. Earl Boykins

    c. Charlie Criss

    d. Tyrone "Muggsy" Bogues

    e. Anthony "Spud" Web

4. Which of these players under 6 feet tall was a team member alongside 7 foot 7 Manute Bol?

    a. Keith "Mister" Jennings

    b. Tyrone "Muggsy" Bogues

    c. Melvin Hirsch

5. How tall was the shortest man to ever play in the NBA?

    a. 5 feet 6 inches

    b. 5 feet 3 inches

    c. 5 feet 7 inches

BONUS

1. What other sports influenced Naismith's design of his basketball game?

    a. Soccer and football

    b. Lacrosse and gymnastics

    c. Duck on a rock and rugby

    d. All of the above

    e. None of the above

2. What was Naismith's job at the YMCA?

    a. Physical education teacher

    b. Youth mentor

    c. Truck driver

3. Which term didn't exist in basketball in 1897?

    a. Foul

    b. Goal

    c. Dribble

    d. Slam dunk

4. How much did the original copy of Dr. James Naismith's 13 rules of basketball sell for in 2010?

    a. $100 million

    b. $7.5 million

    c. $4.3 million

Chapter 2:

Playing Dirty

The first basketball games were extremely aggressive events. Players and spectators were antagonistic and hostile. It was not uncommon to see brawls break out both on and off the court. Spectators threw tomatoes, fruit, and other produce onto the court if they were dissatisfied with a play or a call. If the ball went out of bounds, fans would pick it up and try to keep it. Players, driven to win, would pummel fans to get it back. Aggression was the name of the game.

Roughnecks

Naismith's 13 rules didn't resolve the game's reputation for aggression. As the sport became more popular, audience involvement increased, causing constant chaos which created roughneck players determined to score. In those early games, taking it to the hole could really cost you your soul.

Players past and present are still known for being overly assertive on and off the court. In 2004, Ron Artest of the Indiana Pacers became famous for a brawl reporters called "the malice at the palace"(LQG, 2016). During a play at The Palace stadium in Auburn, Michigan, Artest hit Detroit Pistons' center Ben Wallace in the back of the head. They got into an altercation. When they were pulled apart, a fan threw a cup of Coca-Cola at Artest, who ran into the stands looking for a fight. Fists flew as fans, players, families, referees, and officials alike were engulfed in a full-on brawl. Before all was said and done, there was blood on the floor, bruises, black eyes, and broken bones, just like in Naismith's original games.

Even great players who were known for their charismatic personalities, scoring abilities, and running game were guilty of dangerous play. Kobe Bryant of the Los Angeles Lakers would frequently throw an elbow to the throat or face of anyone who got in his way. He quite often managed to do this with such finesse that cameras rarely caught him. Dikembe Mutombo, a center who played 18 seasons in the NBA on various teams, injured people and left them in need of surgery and stitches. Even the world's best, including Michael Jordan, Julius Erving, and LeBron James, were some of his casualties. Power forward and center Rasheed Wallace accumulated over 300 technical fouls by the time his NBA career ended in 2013. Dennis Rodman had great defensive and rebounding skills. He would also chew you up on the court, literally: He was known for using his elbows, fingernails, and teeth on his opponents.

In the 1980s and early 1990s, the Detroit Pistons were known as the bad boys of basketball. Isiah Thomas, Joe Dumars, Bill Laimbeer, Dennis Rodman, and Rick Mahorn led this very physical team to the championship in 1989 and 1990. The team broke all of rule 12 of that year's official NBA rules regarding unsportsmanlike conduct resulting in a technical foul. This included (Morris, 2014):

- Disrespectfully addressing an official.

- Physically contacting an official.

- Overt actions indicating resentment to a call.

- Use of profanity

- A coach entering onto a court without permission of an official.

- A deliberately thrown elbow or any attempted physical act with no contact.

Basketball has never lost its roughneck quality. As a matter of fact, technical fouls and unsportsmanlike conduct are often indicative of a team's success (Morris, 2014).

Judging by the Court

Different YMCAs had different dimensions for their gymnasiums. If there was less than 1,800 square feet of playing space, you could play a five-man team. If the gymnasium had 1,800 to 3,600 square feet, you would play as many as nine men on each team. The five-man team wasn't established as the norm until 1895 (Logan et al., 2020).

YMCA courts had no specific shape. There could be offices, pillars, and staircases in the way. Balconies overlooked the gymnasium and spectators could actually reach out and interfere with the ball during the game. This problem became so notoriously overwhelming that in 1895, teams were asked to provide a 4-by-6-foot screen to stave off spectator interference (Logan et al., 2020).

Today, basketball courts and equipment follow a particular standard (Logan et al., 2020).

> The standard American basketball court is in the shape of a rectangle 50 feet (15.2 meters) by 94 feet (28.7 meters); high school courts may be slightly smaller. [Court markings include] a center circle, free throw lanes, and a three-point line, that help regulate play. A goal, or basket, 18 inches (46 cm) in diameter is suspended from a backboard at each end of the court. The metal rim of the basket is 10 feet (3 meters) above the floor. In the professional game the backboard is a rectangle, 6 feet (1.8 meters) wide and 3.5 feet (1.1 meters) high, made of a transparent material, usually glass; it may be 4 feet (1.2 meters) high in college. The international court varies somewhat in size and markings. The spherical inflated ball measures 29.5 to 30 inches (74.9 to 76cm) in circumference and weighs 20 to 22 ounces (567 to 624 grams). Its covering is leather or composition.

The creation of wooden backboards was followed by the legalization of glass backboards in 1908–09. Fan-shaped backboards were legalized in 1940–41 (Logan et al., 2020). Today, a team can accrue a technical foul for using the wrong size ball, having the ball inadequately inflated, shattering a backboard, or a coach stepping out of boundary lines.

Stop the Spread

After the first game at the YMCA in Springfield, Massachusetts, Naismith's students got excited. They talked about the game wherever they went. Spectators started showing up in droves. Students staged exhibitions at other schools, YMCAs, and courts across the nation on holidays, and at their jobs. They organized the first teams and leagues.

Basketball's popularity began causing friction at YMCAs used to having 50 or 60 members making use of the gymnasium, with teams accused of monopolizing the space. Games were loud and rowdy, often devolving into violence and animosity between different YMCA branches. New York City and Brooklyn, New York were the primary locations of YMCAs nationwide and the majority of games were played in those areas. The Philadelphia YMCA League was "one of the strongest in the country", yet it was disbanded after other YMCA members "complained that basketball monopolized gym time to the detriment of regular gymnasium work and that it attracted a rowdy, decidedly un-Christian element" (Pro Basketball Encyclopedia, 2023).

Once YMCAs banned basketball, teams began renting halls to play. By 1896, the Amateur Athletic Union (AAU) had taken over responsibility for the games, but their success waned as they constantly battled the blurred lines distinguishing players' amateur, collegiate, and professional status. The AAU also supported popular sports like football and baseball. Basketball, though popular in a few eastern states, wasn't at the top of their list.

World War I helped the spread of the sport. Canada was already playing basketball as the sport's founder and many of the first players were Canadian. Young American men who entered the war played the sport as recreation and taught it to others. Before long, basketball spread across the globe.

[Recovering Scottish soldiers playing basketball with the Women's Army Auxiliary Corp (WAAC).]

Cagers

In 1896, Trenton, New Jersey was the place to be for the first professional caged basketball tournament. Gone were the crate barrel hoops hanging from banisters, fans leaning over balustrades tapping a ball out of range, and food thrown onto the court. There were still plenty of aggressive antics. Unnecessary roughness was expected and even applauded. Skirmishes still occurred, but one significant change was added to address much of the mayhem: A 10–12-foot-high wire-mesh cage.

Balls that went out of bounds were awarded to the first person to recover possession, no matter what team they were on. Before cages, this loose ball, if it happened to land in the laps or between the seats of spectators, could cause an all-out war. Cages kept excited fans safe and allowed the game to progress faster, but spectators could still wreak havoc on a player, much to the enjoyment of the crowd (SI Staff, 1991):

> *Pro basketball in the [19]'20s was no place for shrinking violets. It was considered fair play to drive the man with the ball into the wire or rope, especially if he was shooting. When a home-team player was thus clobbered, it was not unusual for fans to join the resulting fray. The players entered and left the cage through doors at either end, and fans sometimes fought their way in using the same openings.*

Rope netting later replaced the wire mesh but was no less dangerous. A man could go home with just as many rope burns and bruises as he did bloodied wire mesh markings on his arms and back. Joseph K. Schwarzer of the 1919 New York State League claimed his wife thought he had been in a fight when he took his shirt off after a game. Joel S. "Shikey" Gotthoffer, who played professionally in the 1930s with both the Philadelphia Sphas and the Nanticoke in the Penn State League, claimed, "You could play tic tac toe on everybody after a game because the cage marked you up; sometimes you were bleeding and sometimes not. You were like a gladiator, and if you didn't get rid of the ball, you could get killed" (SI Staff, 1991). Strategists like J. Emmett "Flip" Dowling, center in the 1920s New York State League, used the ropes to gather the player with the ball into the net so he couldn't pass it, forcing a jump ball.

These professional gladiator-style games got so brutal, basketball's reputation was damaged to the point where people didn't want to associate themselves with the sport. The athletes themselves were called "cagers" by journalists. Considering that most of these professional games were played in close quarters in church basements, dance halls, and fire houses, officials had to figure out a way to make the game more palatable for the general public. It was time to take basketball from the basement to the next level.

Game Time

How to Play

Divide your group into teams or play one-on-one with a friend. Answer all the *Game Time* questions from the text or your expert knowledge of the game for two points each. Tally up your score at the end of each chapter.

1. What position did Isiah Thomas play?

   a. Small forward

   b. Point guard

   c. Center

2. Which Piston's 1986 second-round pick was one of the bad boys?

   a. John Salley

   b. Dennis Rodman

   c. Chauncey Robinson

3. True or False: Isiah Thomas won his first championship in 1989.

4. True or False: Isiah Thomas was the second pick in the 1981 NBA draft.

5. Who won the NBA Championship in 1989 between the Los Angeles Lakers and the Detroit Pistons?

6. Which team started 1989–90 with an NBA Championship win?

    a. Chicago Bulls

    b. Los Angeles Lakers

    c. Detroit Pistons

7. In today's game, can you get a technical foul for wearing the wrong head- or wristband?

    a. Yes, if the referee catches it and the coach doesn't correct it before the game.

    b. No, you don't get technical fouls for dress codes.

8. Can you get a technical foul for flipping off a referee from the bench during a game?

    a. Yes

    b. No

9. Which international event significantly impacted the spread of basketball in the 1900s?

    a. New technology

    b. World War I

    c. The extended use of electricity

10. Which basketball organization took over collegiate sports in 1896?

    a. AAU

    b. ABA

    c. NBL

11. The dimensions of today's NBA court are:

    a. 84 by 50 feet

    b. 94 feet by 50 feet

    c. 92 feet by 49 feet

12. True or False: Caged games were played at both the collegiate and professional levels.

Chapter 3:

Next Level

From the 1890s through around 1910, Naismith continued perfecting his game. The peach basket was exchanged for a macrame net and metal rim around 1912–13. A pole was added to the basket so the game could be played outdoors. The soccer ball was retired and a new laced-up basketball was created by A.G. Spalding and Brothers. The 30-inch molded Spalding ball became the official basketball in 1940–41 (Logan et al., 2020). Spalding is still the official basketball in use by all NBA and Women's National Basketball Association (WNBA) professional basketball teams in the United States today.

As the game changed, so did the players. The first team to draw national attention was the 23rd Street, New York YMCA team featuring Sandy Shields, John Wendelken, and Kid Abadie, winning 48 out of 49 games in two seasons (Pro Basketball Encyclopedia, 2023). Kid Abadie, whose formal name was Alfred Camile Abadie, was 5 foot 11 inches and weighed in at 165 pounds. He had no college education and was 18 years old when he started playing for the New York YMCA team. At 21, he played guard and center with the New York Wanderers, scoring an average of 3 points per game (Pro Basketball Encyclopedia, 2023). Wendelken, a Columbia University medical student, was the star center for the Wanderers, scoring an average of 5.9 points per game. He started with the 23rd Street YMCA and continued under the auspices of the AAU at age 19. When the 23rd Street team became the independent Wanderers in 1897, he was still on the roster (Pro Basketball Encyclopedia, 2023).

Sandy Shields, originally a trained gymnast, was one of the sleekest, fastest, strongest, and most aggressive men on the 23rd Street team. He retired at 20 years old from the Wanderers even though he had the highest scoring average of the three at 9.8 points per game (Pro Basketball Encyclopedia, 2023). He was actress Brooke Shields' great grandfather.

Winning teams tended to have taller players. In 1947, the average height of a male professional basketball player was 6 feet 2 inches. In 2019, the NBA ruled the exact height of players had to be taken and recorded by team physicians. For some players, inflating those stats was beneficial. Kevin Durant, who played for both the Golden State Warriors and the Brooklyn Nets in 2019, felt pigeonholing him based on his size could keep him from playing the positions and the game he wanted to play (Li, 2019). In high school his height was recorded at 6 feet 9 inches tall. In a 2016 interview with the *Wall Street Journal* he quipped, "When I'm talking to women, I'm 7 feet. In basketball circles, I'm 6–9" (Li, 2019).

Today, a 7-foot player is almost the norm. Sudanese American Manute Bol stood 7 feet 7 inches tall with a wingspan of 8 feet 6 inches. You couldn't get much of anything past him. He was a blocking machine, ramping up 2,086 blocked shots over his career (Dougherty, 2020). Bol's counterpart was Gheorghe Mureşan, who measured Bol's exact height. They both played for the Washington Bullets at one time in their careers. Kareem Abdul Jabbar, Tacko Fall, Yao Ming, Shawn Bradley, Mark Eaton, Rik Smits, Ralph Sampson, Boban Marjanović, and Zydrunas "Big Z" Ilgauskas are all over 7 feet tall, with Jabbar being the shortest at 7 feet 1 ½ inches.

A college education, or any education at all, was not a prerequisite for playing in amateur leagues. In the early days, you could play college and professional basketball at the same time, or play under an assumed name. You didn't have to have a sterling reputation and the lines between professional and amateur were not well defined. Home teams could choose between playing four 10-minute quarters or three 15-minute periods.

Today's game typically takes 2 to 3 hours to finish, depending on the number of delays for fouls, feuds, time-outs, and other mishaps. Players must have at least a high school diploma and be 19 years of age to play professionally. Height is preferred, but not required.

Expansion and Great Expectations

By 1895, basketball had become an established sport at both men's and women's high schools. The Amateur Athletic Union (AAU), the frontrunner for collegiate sports, staged the first basketball tournament in 1897. New York City's 23rd Street YMCA, later known as the Wanderers, won the title. The Wanderers were the first independent professional team. Having no backing from the amateur, collegiate, or professional ranks, they wandered from place to place playing wherever there was accommodation and payment. "Independent" meant teams had to depend on themselves for everything from uniforms to transportation, room and board, marketing, and venues.

Unlike basketball, football was very popular in the United States in the 1900s, but it was also an extremely dangerous sport, much more so than basketball. In its early days, there were no hard helmets to protect fragile brains. Life-altering injuries and even death were common. In 1905, President Theodore Roosevelt sought to ban college football because of its potential for life-threatening injuries. This edict met with several protests. Roosevelt responded by demanding colleges form a council that could improve the sport and reduce injuries. The National Collegiate Athletic Association (NCAA) was originally formed to find ways to make football safer, but eventually took over the organization of all collegiate sports, including basketball.

In 1898, Naismith's friend Emil Liston started a basketball team at the University of Kansas. They played YMCA teams until 1901, when more collegiate teams were established. By 1907, Naismith was employed as a coach for the University of Kansas. Ironically, the game's inventor had the worst losing streak in the history of the team losing 59 of 60 games (MDJ, 2019).

Expansion of the sport at a national level took place in the 1920s, with small leagues of two or three professional and amateur teams popping up in different states. Because playing standards were still relatively lax concerning what constituted amateur and professional in the 1930s, the AAU had a hard time separating the amateur players from the professionals. Having a seasoned professional on an amateur team gave that team an unfair advantage.

Blackballed

The first professional basketball league, formed in 1898, was the National Basketball League (NBL), which consisted of six Northeastern teams (Basketball.org, n.d.):

- New York Wanderers

- Trenton Nationals

- Millville Glass Blowers

- Bristol Pile Drivers

- Camden Skeeters

- Pennsylvania Bicycle Club

The Black community, however, wasn't introduced to basketball until 1904 when physical education teacher and educator Edward Bancroft shared it with his physical education students in Washington, D.C. He learned about the game and how to play it while studying at Harvard University. The game then spread across New York, Philadelphia, Baltimore, and other areas on the east coast.

In 1907, the Smart Set Athletic Club of Brooklyn, New York formed the first organized, independent black basketball team in the US (Gay, 2021). More teams formed as the game gained notoriety in the black community, but segregation kept many of them from access to gyms and other venues where white teams played. This, however, did not stop their progress. They played in church basements, armories, and dance ballrooms. Professional performers, singers, musicians, and promoters would link up with these teams and put together sold-out shows around them. As ticket sales took off, so did the game's popularity.

The most successful team during this era was the Harlem Rens, founded, owned, and coached by artist and Philadelphia activist Robert Douglas. In New York, Douglas was called "the Father of Black Basketball" by his contemporaries and those he coached. His team won 88 consecutive games in the 1932–33 season. In the '20s and early '30s, their matches against the Celtics were legendary. The Harlem Rens played anyone, Black or White. In 1938, they were invited to the World Basketball Tournament, the first of its kind. There were 10 teams in the lineup. The Harlem Globetrotters was the only other "Black Five," the term used for an all-Black team, in the tournament. The Rens won the tournament in 1939, lost to the Globetrotters in 1940, and finished second to the Minneapolis Lakers in 1948 (Harlem World Magazine, 2019).

Integration's door opened slowly. The NBL began hiring Black players in 1942. These athletes played for the Chicago Studebakers and Toledo's Jim White Chevrolets. Black Five teams also paved the way, leaving a legacy of commitment, strength, and triumph for black players.

The ball in basketball is neither black nor white. It doesn't have a nationality or religion. It's a game that anyone can play, and those who loved the sport and worked at it, no matter their race, became champions.

The Harlem Globetrotters and Their Contribution to Professional Basketball

The Harlem Globetrotters was a Black Five team founded in Chicago in 1926 during the Harlem Renaissance. They were originally formed as an exhibition team called the Savoy Big Five that played as a precursor to dance socials at the Savoy Ballroom in Harlem. Most of the players came from Wendell Phillips High School on the south side of Chicago.

The Harlem Globetrotters brought style and flash to the game. On one hand they were professionals playing serious ball. On the other hand they were entertainers exhibiting deliriously funny antics, crazy shots, and insane footwork. "They were a highly competitive team popularizing the slam dunk, the fast break, emphasizing the forward and point guard positions, and the figure-eight weave" (Grove, 2021). In 1940 they won the World Professional Basketball Tournament, competing against all-White teams. In 1948, they defeated the Minneapolis Lakers, an all-White NBL team, in the same tournament.

Their success was not without its trials. Jim Horne, who played with the Globetrotters in the 1950s, said "We were entertaining people and still being treated less than human. In the South, we couldn't eat in most places and we had to stay in the worst hotels. Coming from Buffalo, New York, it was a rude awakening. It was rough in those days" (Grove, 2021).

The Globetrotters' roster contained such notables as Wilt "The Stilt" Chamberlain, Nat "Sweetwater" Clifton, Connie "The Hawk" Hawkins, Meadowlark Lemon, Fred "Curly" Neal, Reece "Goose" Tatum, Marques Haynes, "Wee" Willie Gardner, and Lynette Woodard—the first woman to ever play on the team.

In 1982, the Harlem Globetrotters received a well deserved star on the Hollywood Walk of Fame. Whenever you see silky smooth finger rolls, tantalizing tricks, high-flying jump shots, dastardly dunks, and incredible style you can thank the Harlem Globetrotters for introducing this style of fiery fun, fancy footwork, and fantastic finesse to the game.

Color-Blind

Black players were not allowed in the NBA when it was established in 1949. Charles "Chuck" Cooper, Nat "Sweetwater" Clifton, and Earl Francis "Big Cat" Lloyd pioneered Black inclusion. Cooper, who played for the Harlem Globetrotters straight out of college in 1950, was the first African American ever drafted to an NBA team, on April 25, 1950. He was the 13th overall pick and the first pick of the second round for the Boston Celtics (Aschburner, 2022). The 6 feet 5 inch, 205-pound player attended West Virginia State and Duquesne Universities. He played for 6 years as a small forward and a shooting guard (Wikipedia Contributors, 2020).

Nat "Sweetwater" Clifton played for the Harlem Globetrotters, and also played professional baseball. He signed with the New York Knicks on May 24, 1950 as a power forward (Aschburner, 2022). He was the first African American to sign an NBA contract. He acquired his nickname as a child because he was kind and loved sweet soft drinks. While racism's thorny edges pricked him during and after a game, he remained a tough and tender leader on and off the court.

Earl Francis "Big Cat" Lloyd was the first African American to actually play in an official capacity in an NBA game. Lloyd played as a member of the starting lineup for the Washington Capitols on October 31, 1950 (Aschburner, 2022). He was drafted and served in the military in 1951, returning to the NBA in 1952. His career took off from there (The HistoryMakers, 2019):

> *Lloyd and teammate Jim Tucker became the first African Americans to win an NBA title in 1955 with Dolph Schayes and the Syracuse Nationals. That year, Lloyd averaged 10.2 points and 7.7 rebounds for Syracuse, beating the Fort Wayne Pistons four games to three in a seven game series for the NBA title. Lloyd closed out his playing career with the Detroit Pistons from 1958 to 1960. Over his professional career, Lloyd played in over 560 games in nine seasons and averaged 8.4 points and 6.4 rebounds per game.*

Cooper, Clifton, and Lloyd paved the way for greats like Bill Russell and Wilt Chamberlain. Russell was drafted by the Boston Celtics in 1956, and was named the NBA's first superstar player alongside George Mikan. Chamberlain was drafted by the Philadelphia Warriors in 1959.

Lloyd, Clifton, and Cooper looked out for one another, especially when they were on the road. They shared information regarding where it was safe to eat, sleep, find entertainment, and spend the night. They were strong, inspiring, and professional on and off the court. All three men were inducted into the Naismith Hall of Fame. They changed the way the world saw professional basketball, and, in a game of skill, talent, wit, leadership, and power, spectators eventually became more color-blind.

Game Time

How to Play

Divide your group into teams or play one-on-one with a friend. Answer all the *Game Time* questions from the text and your basketball knowledge for two points each. Test your basketball trivia expertise by answering the bonus questions for three points each. Tally up your score at the end of each chapter.

1. What was Wilt Chamberlain's nickname?

    a. Magic

    b. Wilt the Stilt

    c. He didn't have one

2. Which of these NBA greats retired in 1989?

    a. Kareem Abdul-Jabbar

b. Wilt Chamberlain

c. Bill Russell

3. Which of the original Globetrotters also became one of the first African American basketball players to sign on with an NBA team in April 1950?

a. Jim Horn

b. Charles Cooper

c. Wilt Chamberlain

d. Meadowlark Lemon

4. Which basketball brand is used exclusively by the NBA?

a. Wilson

b. Molton

c. Spalding

5. What was the name of the Philadelphia team that drafted Wilt Chamberlain in 1959?

a. Philadelphia 76ers

b. Harlem Globetrotters

c. Philadelphia Warriors

d. Syracuse Nationals

BONUS

1. What number did Kareem Adbul-Jabbar wear?

a. 10

b. 17

c. 33

2. Kareem Abdul-Jabbar won his last NBA MVP in:

a. 1980

b. 1983

c. 1987

Chapter 4:

The Ball's in Your Court

In the 1920s, '30s, and '40s, when everything was scarce, money played a major role in the advancement of amateur and professional basketball. The power of the NCAA was growing to the point of pushing the AAU into the background. The money generated by NCAA games began to attract illegal gambling. Before television, teams traveled to play games and being there live was the only way you could see them. Madison Square Garden hosted thousands of games and was the favorite place in the United States for gambling rings to conduct business, especially in the postwar era of the 1950s. Collegiate athletes weren't getting paid, but owners, mobsters, and certain fans were making huge amounts of money.

The NBL obtained sponsorships and funding from large corporations like General Motors. They paid players up to $55,000. By 1949, "George Mikan was making $60,000 plus incentives to play for the Chicago American Gears" (McMahon, 2021). The disparity between pro player salaries and college players' empty pockets set the stage for some double dealing.

Gambling and the Evolution of College Basketball

The more attention and income the game generated, the more mobsters and gamblers were drawn to it. The larger the crowd, the more money there was to be made. Coaches who had never recruited before began to scout out high school basketball games for the best players. They wanted to win. Winning meant status, and money in their pockets too.

By 1950, organized crime had taken over illegal gambling in New York state and on most of the east coast. A few teams in the south also fell prey to the sports gambling phenomenon. Eddie Guard, who played for Long Island University (LIU), was looking for a way to make a quick buck. College players were drawing crowds night after night to huge venues like Madison Square Garden. Times were hard. Money was tight. Enterprising Eddie sought out Salvatore Sollazzo, a Sicilian jeweler, gambler, and money man, to help him set up a point-shaving scheme. Guard recruited men from his team and from teams he played against, including eight City College of New York (CCNY) players, convincing them that they could make thousands of dollars in cash on the side if they cooperated with him and Sallazo.

LIU's forward Sherman White was heavily recruited by the two men. Originally from Philadelphia, Pennsylvania, White was one of the few Black players on the LIU team. He was also the leading scorer in the NCAA. Hal Uplinger, who played guard for LIU alongside White, said, "I have seen only two ball players equal to White—Michael Jordan and Kobe Bryant" (Gildea, 2011). Sadly, despite his many talents, White would never get to accomplish his dream of playing with the NBA. After a lot of steak and lobster dinners, and money on the table, he was persuaded to take part in Guard and Saollazo's scheme.

By the end of 1950, Guard had recruited over 80 men from Kentucky University, Bradley University, several colleges and universities in New York, and others in Illinois and in the southern states. Most of the players who joined these ranks were Whites.

Then, in 1951, Junius Kellogg, a young Black athlete, was asked to take a bribe from a White player who was a blatant racist and who had never spoken to him before. Kellogg, wary of this sudden friendliness, refused the money and told his coach about it. He was the college's first Black scholarship candidate; he wasn't taking any chances. His coach advised him to report the incident to the New York City District Attorney's office. An investigation followed, finding "32 players from seven colleges who took bribes to fix 86 games in 17 states between 1947 and 1950" (Litsky, 1998). Arrests occurred immediately. When the scandal broke, it changed college basketball forever.

The fallout for colleges hit CCNY the hardest. They were stripped of their Division I status and relegated to a Division III school. They remain in Division III to this day. Six of the CCNY players were suspended. Sollazzo got 12 years in prison for gambling and tax evasion. Eddie Guard got off lightly with 3 years, serving only 9 months. Though he was the ringleader, he was praised by the District Attorney for cooperating with the authorities. The Kentucky players all got off scot-free. Sherman White, the Black player who some said would have otherwise ended up in Naismith's Hall of Fame, served a year in Rikers Island maximum-security prison, known for its malicious treatment of prisoners, and was never allowed to play the sport he loved again.

Television's Influence

Basketball first spread by word of mouth. Newspapers, magazines, journals, and other printed publications were the primary media of the day when the sport was invented. Initially, there weren't enough people paying attention to basketball to warrant mass media coverage. Interest in the sport grew largely because of the advent of television in 1939.

The first basketball game ever viewed on television was between Pittsburgh and Fordham University at Madison Square Garden. It was aired on February 28, 1940 by NBC on W2XBS, now known as WNBC or Channel 4 New York (Hermann, 2022). Not much is known about that early broadcast because not many people thought it was important enough to watch. The country was still reeling from the Great Depression, so most people couldn't afford the luxury of a television.

By 1963, however, NCAA championship games, especially those held in March, were broadcasting on networks worldwide and raking in the big bucks. By the 1980s, "rights fees for these games soared from a few million dollars to well over $50 million. As for broadcasting the NCAA finals, a television contract that began in 2003 gave the NCAA an average of $545 million per year" (Pro Basketball Encyclopedia, 2023). These lucrative television network contracts increased visibility for both men's and women's college basketball, offering colleges more money to recruit, house, and provide tuition for athletes. Revenue from television also paved the way for top-tier college athletes to begin earning money from endorsements.

Dribbling for Dollars

The National Association of Intercollegiate Athletics (NAIA) hosted the first national college tournament in 1937. At that time, college athletes were receiving academic scholarships, but they were not making any money, despite their hard work and dedication. Fast forward to 2017 when 82% of the NCAA's revenue came from Division I basketball. Today, NCAA revenue tops the charts at billions of dollars per year.

[Florida State University basketball player circa 1958.]

According to the NCAA 2022 financial report (NCAA, 2022):

> *About 60% of the NCAA's annual revenue—around $600 million—is annually distributed directly to Division I member schools and conferences, while more than $150 million funds Division I championships. Divisions II and III receive 4.37% and 3.18% of all NCAA revenue, respectively, which both divisions divide to fund their championships and support their membership. The NCAA also funds several services and educational programs for student-athletes and member schools, as well as a number of scholarship, grant, and internship programs.*

"March Madness" is the most lucrative collegiate basketball season. In March 2019, advertisers spent over $900 million to promote their products during March Madness (Majidi, 2023). This single elimination tournament involves 68 teams that compete in seven rounds for the national championship. The "Final Four" compete in two single elimination games, with the winning teams then competing for the title. With the title comes prestige, additional revenue and endorsements for the winning college, and more ability for the players to make money through the use of their name and image.

Television changed the focus of the game professionally and at the collegiate level. Teams were essentially dribbling for dollars and, for some, it was a win–win situation. Tom King of the Detroit Falcons was paid $16,500 in 1946–47. His job included playing basketball and working in the front office as a business and publicity director. Even though he averaged only 5.1 points per game, he was paid more than anyone else. Joe Fulks, "averaged 22.3 points per game for Philadelphia and was paid $8,000." The average player made $4,000 to $5,000 per contract year. (McMahon, 2021). Fast forward to today's game where college athletes can now benefit from endorsements. NBA players like Michael Jordan, Julius Erving, and Wilt Chamberlain had to earn their place and salaries. NBA drafts now sign multi-million dollar contracts with young athletes before they play a single game. Basketball has become a very lucrative business.

Game Time

How to Play

Divide your group into teams or play one-on-one with a friend. Answer all the *Game Time* questions from the text or your knowledge of basketball for two points each. Test your basketball trivia expertise by answering the bonus questions for three points each. Tally up your score at the end of each chapter.

1. Who staged their first collegiate basketball tournament in 1937?

   a. The AAU

   b. The NAIA

   c. The NBL

2. Why didn't the print media promote the first televised basketball game?

   a. Because there weren't enough teams playing.

   b. Because television wasn't as fun as being at the game.

   c. Because most people couldn't afford a television.

   d. Because the game wasn't that popular.

3. Which of these organizations benefited most from the advent of American television?

   a. The AAU

   b. The AST

   c. The NAIA

d. The NCAA

4. Why was television so important to college basketball?

    a. Advertising dollars

    b. Visibility

    c. None of the above

    d. A and B

5. Who was the highest paid player in 1946–47?

    a. George Mikan

    b. Joe Fulks

    c. Tom King

6. Which exceptional player lost his entire career and credibility due to gambling?

    a. Eddie Guard

    b. Sherman White

    c. Junius Kellogg

BONUS

1. How many 3-pointers did Kareem Abdul-Jabbar make in his career?

2. Which team is the oldest NBA franchise?

    a. Lakers

    b. 76ers

c. Bucks

d. Pistons

Chapter 5:

Rivals

The Basketball Association of America (BAA) emerged as a rival to the NBL in the 1940s under the auspices of prominent businessman and owner of the Boston Gardens, Walter Brown. Brown observed the NBL's growth and surmised there was money to be made. He was already hosting hockey games at the garden, and looked forward to making money in the off-season hosting basketball games.

The NBL and the BAA battled it out from 1946 to 1949. The Los Angeles Lakers, once known as the Minneapolis Lakers, and the Rochester Royals, now the Sacramento Kings, both joined the BAA in 1948–49. The Philadelphia 76ers (formerly the Syracuse Nationals), the Detroit Pistons (formerly the Fort Wayne Zollner Pistons), and the Atlanta Hawks (formerly the Tri-City Black Hawks) joined the NBA when the NBL merged with the BAA in 1949.

From Auditoriums to Stadiums

Brown expected the BAA to easily replace the NBL, but things didn't go as planned. Though the BAA boasted larger venues, the NBL still boasted the best players and coaches. After three years of competing, the BAA and NBL team owners decided to work together. They met in New York City to discuss a merger.

The NBL had more leagues than the BAA. The BAA wanted the deal recorded as an expansion, claiming that they were merely expanding the number of teams they owned. The NBL, however, considered it a merger. The two sides came to an agreement. On paper, the deal was called an expansion. Unfortunately, this meant the history of many of the NBL players was erased as, officially, NBA history began with the BAA in 1946. African Americans who had once played for the NBL were completely shut out, as Blacks weren't allowed to play in the new NBA. Once the NBL was dissolved, so were their professional careers.

Walter Brown hired his first Black player, Chuck Cooper, from Duquesne University in 1950. A rival owner said, "Don't you know he's colored?" to which Brown responded, "I don't care if he's striped, plaid, or polka dot" (Aschburner, 2022). Brown was a businessman. He and his coach recognized that in order to be the best team, you had to hire the best players. It didn't matter to him what color they were because the money he made was always green.

NBA—The Final Frontier

When the smoke cleared, the NBA was the only professional league in North America. The American Basketball Association (ABA), commissioned by George Mikan, rose up to compete against the NBA in 1967–68. The ABA started with 11 teams: the New Jersey Americans, Anaheim Amigos, New Orleans Buccaneers, Dallas Chaparrals, Kentucky Colonels, Houston Mavericks, Minnesota Muskies, Oakland Oaks, Indiana Pacers, Pittsburgh Pipers, and Denver Rockets. The two leagues feuded bitterly over available college athletes.

The ABA folded in 1976 due to its inability to pay expensive league fees. Four of its teams were taken into the NBA-the Denver Nuggets (formerly the Rockets), San Antonio Spurs, Indiana Pacers, and the New York Nets (now the Brooklyn Nets). Julius Irving played for the Nets. His contract was sold to the 76ers in the merger. He is the only player to have ever won an MVP in the ABA and the NBA.

The NBA currently comprises 30 teams in the United States and one in Canada. They play in athletic stadiums to millions of spectators live, on television, and streaming all over the world. By 1949, American professional basketball had finally found a permanent home.

Game Time

How to Play

Divide your group into teams or play one-on-one with a friend. Answer all the *Game Time* questions from the text or your basketball knowledge for two points each. Test your basketball trivia expertise by answering the bonus questions for three points each. Tally up your score at the end of each chapter.

1. Which team was named by a contest winner as part of an Independence Day celebration?

    a. Warriors

    b. 76ers

    c. Eagles

2. Which team was originally called the Syracuse Nationals?

    a. Pistons

    b. Nuggets

    c. Knicks

    d. 76ers

3. This rival association, developed in 1967–68, was the NBA's nemesis for 4 years.

    a. The BAA

    b. The ABA

    c. The AAU

4. What was the original name of the Los Angeles Lakers?

    a. The Portsmouth Lakers

    b. The Sacramento Lakers

    c. The Minneapolis Lakers

5. Who is the only player to win "Most Valuable Player" (MVP) awards in the ABA and NBA?

    a. Clyde Drexler

    b. Kevin McHale

    c. Julius Erving

BONUS

1. What is the name of the league that the NBA launched to develop young players?

    a. The NBDL

    b. The ABA

    c. The LLDT

2. Which set of teams is part of the Eastern Conference Atlantic Division?

    a. Boston Celtics, Philadelphia 76ers, Toronto Raptors

    b. Sacramento Kings, New York Knicks, Memphis Grizzlies

    c. Washington Wizards, Boston Celtics, Brooklyn Nets

    d. Golden State Warriors, Chicago Bulls, Cleveland Cavaliers

3. What was the name of the team that was originally named after the businessman who owned them?

    a. 76ers

    b. Pistons

    c. Hawks

Chapter 6:

We Are the Champions

Between 1930 and 1936, the game Naismith had created as a distraction had traveled the world. Eight countries came together to form the International Basketball Federation (FIBA) for players overseas. Basketball also found a spot in the 1936 Olympic Games. Cable television in the 1980s took the game to another level. Star players like Earvin "Magic" Johnson, Julius "Dr. J." Erving, and Michael "Air" Jordan increased excitement and exposure, moving basketball to the forefront of American sports.

The Chosen Ones

The NBA draft began in 1947. Coaches and owners could draft college and high school students 18 years of age and older through a lottery system. Kobe Bryant, LeBron James, Kevin Garnett, Dwight Howard, Tracy McGrady, and Amar'e Stoudemire were all drafted straight out of high school.

Draft years considered the most notable were 1984, 1996, and 2003. Hakeem Olajuwon, Michael Jordan, and Charles Barkley were drafted in 1984. They were also on the list of top 10 picks that year which included Sam Bowie, Sam Perkins, Melvin Turpin, Alvin Robertson, Lancaster Gordon, and Otis Thorpe. Most Valuable Player (MVP) All-Star players Allen Iverson, Steve Nash, and Kobe Bryant were drafted in 1996. Superstars LeBron James, Dwyane Wade, Carmelo Anthony, and Chris Bosh were drafted in 2003.

The 14 teams that don't make the playoffs get to participate in a lottery, usually held in May. Each team is assigned a numbered ball according to their record. The team with the worst record, for example, is assigned the number one. Ping pong balls marked 1–14 are spun around for 20 seconds. The first ball drawn is the team that will have the first pick in the NBA draft. This can get complicated when the draft pick is owned by another team.

What Makes a Championship Team?

Drafting excellent players and paying big money doesn't guarantee a winning team. Five prominent factors recognized in championship teams like the Los Angeles Lakers, Golden State Warriors, Boston Celtics, Chicago Bulls, and San Antonio Spurs are:

- Coaches who are adept at choosing, training, and leading players.

- Players with basketball intelligence. They are well-versed in all the dynamics of how the game is played.

- Defenders who know how to operate on the perimeter, play both ends of the court, and can present an intimidating presence in the paint.

- Accurate free throw shooters, layup artists, and a team who knows how to find and connect with them.

- A closer who is dependable and reliable in any crunch time situation.

Team chemistry is also essential for a championship team. Superstars don't necessarily make super teams. Scottie Pippen, Hakeem Olajuwon, and Charles Barkley all had celebrity status but did not play well together on the 1998–99 Houston Rockets. Steve Nash and Dwight Howard joined the Los Angeles Lakers lineup in 2012–13 to add defensive and offensive power to the team. Both men suffered multiple injuries that affected the team chemistry and kept them out of the championship. Injuries, missed free throws, and super egos were responsible for the 1994–95 Orlando Magic losses that featured Shaquille O'Neal, Anfernee Hardaway, and Nick Anderson. Champions Stephen Curry, Giannis Antetokounmpo, and LeBron James all credit, trust, and rely on their teammates for their successes. But even the Greatest of All Time (GOAT) LeBron James failed to deliver on his promise to win a championship game for the Miami Heat in the 2010–11 season when he played with Dwyane Wade and Chris Bosh.

Chemistry is that undeniable synchronicity that happens when leaders, players, and team management come together as a single unit. Unity, focus, and commitment to a team vision coupled with talent, skill, and training wins championships.

Top 10 Championship Teams of All Time

There are several different schools of thought on who was the greatest team of all time. According to a September 2011 *Bleacher Report* (Imaz, 2011), the following teams were top 10 champions.

Team	Year	Record	Talent	Coach
Chicago Bulls	1995–96	72–10	Ron Harper, Michael Jordan, Scottie Pippen, Dennis Rodman, Luc Longley, Steve Kerr, Randy Brown, Toni Kukoč, Jud Buechler, John Salley, Bill Wennington	Phil Jackson
Los Angeles Lakers	1986–87	65–17	Magic Johnson, James Worthy, Kareem Abdul-Jabbar, Byron Scott, A.C. Green, Michael Cooper, Mychal Thompson, Kurt Rambis	Pat Riley
Boston	1985–86	67–15	Larry Bird,	K.C. Jones

Team	Year	Record	Talent	Coach
Celtics			Kevin McHale, Dennis Johnson, Danny Ainge, Robert Parish	

Team	Year	Record	Talent	Coach
Los Angeles Lakers	1971–72	69–13	Jerry West, Elgin Baylor, Wilt Chamberlain, Gail Goodrich, Happy Hairston	Bill Sharman
Detroit Pistons	1988–89	63–19	Dennis Rodman, John Salley, Bill Laimbeer, Isiah Thomas, Joe Dumars, Mark Aguirre	Chuck Daly
Chicago Bulls	1996–97	69–13	Michael Jordan, Scottie Pippin, Toni Kukoč, Luc Longley, Dennis Rodman	Phil Jackson
Milwaukee Bucks	1970–71	66–16	Oscar Robertson, Kareem Abdul-Jabbar, Bob Dandridge, Jon McGlocklin, Greg Smith	Larry Costello
Philadelphia	1982–83	65–17	Julius Erving,	Billy

Team	Year	Record	Talent	Coach
76ers			Andrew Toney, Maurice Cheeks, Moses Malone, Bobby Jones	Cunningham

Team	Year	Record	Talent	Coach
Chicago Bulls	1991–92	67–15	Michael Jordan, Scottie Pippin, Horace Grant, B.J. Armstrong, Craig Hodges, John Paxson, Stacey King, Will Perdue	Phil Jackson
Boston Celtics	1964–65	62–18	Bill Russell, Sam Jones, John Havlicek	Red Auerbach

In 2020, however, the scoreboard changed. According to *Lineups* (Worthington, 2020), the Chicago Bulls maintained their status as number one, but the number two spot was taken by the Golden State Warriors led by coach Steve Kerr.

Team	Season	Record	Leading Scorer/PPG	Playoff Result
Bulls	1995–96	72–10	Michael Jordan (30.4)	NBA Finals Champions
Warriors	2016–17	67–15	Stephen Curry (25.3)	NBA Finals Champions
Lakers	1971–72	69–13	Gail Goodrich (25.9)	NBA Finals Champions
Celtics	1985–86	67–15	Larry Bird (25.8)	NBA Finals Champions

Team	Season	Record	Leading Scorer/PPG	Playoff Result
Bulls	1996–97	69–13	Michael Jordan (29.6)	NBA Finals Champions
76ers	1966–67	68–13	Wilt Chamberlain (24.1)	NBA Finals Champions
Bucks	1970–71	66–16	Kareem Abdul-Jabbar (31.7)	NBA Finals Champions
Lakers	1986–87	65–17	Magic Johnson (23.9)	NBA Finals Champions
Spurs	1998–99	37–13	Tim Duncan (21.7)	NBA Finals Champions
Lakers	2000–01	56–26	Shaquille O'Neal (28.7)	NBA Finals Champions

According to NBA playoff statistics for 2022–23, the following is true (NBA, 2023):

- Milwaukee Bucks lead with most points in a game at 138.

- Golden State Warriors lead with most rebounds and most assists in a game at 59 and 38, respectively.

- Most steals in a game are tied between the Denver Nuggets, Golden State Warriors, New York Knicks, and Philadelphia 76ers at 14.

- Most three-pointers in a game goes to the Milwaukee Bucks at 25, with the Golden State Warriors, Boston Celtics, and Philadelphia 76ers tied at 21.

- The Philadelphia 76ers have the highest free throw percentage at 88.6.

- The Warriors get top billing for assists percentage at 28.2.

- The Sacramento Kings win first place for rebounds per game at 47.7.

Game Time

How to Play

Divide your group into teams or play one-on-one with a friend. Answer all the *Game Time* questions from the text or your basketball knowledge for two points each. Test your basketball trivia expertise by answering the bonus questions for three points each. Tally up your score at the end of each chapter.

1. Which coach dominated the NBA in 1991–92 and 1995–97?

    a. Steve Kerr

    b. Phil Jackson

    c. Pat Riley

2. What team did Michael Jordan play for?

    a. Bucks

    b. Cavaliers

    c. Bulls

3. What team did Yao Ming play for?

    a. Rockets

    b. Spurs

    c. Cavaliers

4. Larry Bird played for which team his entire career?

    a. Celtics

    b. Bucks

    c. Nets

5. What current coach played for the 1995–96 championship Bulls?

    a. Toni Kukoč

    b. Billy Schmidt

    c. Steve Kerr

BONUS:

1. Based on the top 10 charts, which team could be considered a dynasty team?

    a. Bulls

    b. 76ers

    c. Rockets

2. Which player was rookie of the year for the 1979–80 season?

a. Chris Bosh

b. Larry Bird

c. Julius Erving

3. Where did Hakeem Olajuwon play college basketball?

    a. Duke University

    b. University of Florida

    c. University of Houston

    d. Central Arkansas

    e. University of Kentucky

4. Which two NBA international players were originally from Australia?

    a. Kyrie Irving and Andrew Bogut

    b. Andrew Wiggins and Andrew Bogut

    c. Andrea Bargnani and Chris Bosh

5. What pick was Kobe Bryant in the first round draft of 1996?

    a. 5

    b. 10

    c. 13

    d. 15

Chapter 7:

Dynasty and Legacy

An NBA dynasty is a team that dominates in playoffs and finals, winning consecutive championships with the same or similar team roster. The road to an NBA dynasty is fraught with the perils of injuries, trades, failed attempts, and losses. It takes teamwork, great coaching, hard work, grit, preparation, adaptation, and insight for a franchise to earn the dynasty crown. Only a few have ever achieved this level in the history of the NBA.

NBA Dynasties Past and Present

First on the list is the undeniable 1990–98 Chicago Bulls, winning six consecutive championship rings. The dynamic duo of Scottie Pippen and Michael Jordan took the Bulls to two "three-peat" (McGregor, 2022) finals, giving them six-for-six championship titles. Despite internal discord and differences in 1997–98, the Bulls won a staggering 72 games in one season, clearing the finals hurdle with a win. "The Bulls denied so many worthy franchises of opportunities to win titles and were never truly dethroned, which is the ultimate measure of an unstoppable dynasty" (McGregor, 2022).

From 1979 to 1989, the Los Angeles Lakers took eight trips to the finals, winning five championship rings. Nicknamed "Showtime" (McGregor, 2022), this Lakers team starred Magic Johnson and Kareem Abdul-Jabbar. Powerhouses James Worthy, Byron Scott, Bob McAdoo, and coach Pat Riley joined the team later. This team secured a "decade of dominance" (McGregor, 2022).

From 1957 to 1969, the Boston Celtics won 11 out of 12 championships, including winning eight in a row. Their legendary roster included Bill Russell, Bob Cousy, John Havlicek, Tom Heinsohn, and Sam Jones. They nailed their dynasty spot with wins against "all-time greats like Paul Arizin, Wilt Chamberlain, Oscar Robertson, Bob Pettit, Elgin Baylor and Jerry West, among others" (McGregor, 2022).

Coming in at number four on the list is the revolutionary Golden State Warriors. The Warriors earned dynasty status in 2018 when they won the finals over the Cleveland Cavaliers in a clean sweep, and went on to win three back-to-back titles in 4 years. The dream team consisted of the "Splash Brothers", Steph Curry and Klay Thompson; Kevin Durant, nicknamed "Durantula" and the "Slim Reaper;" and the aggressive defender Draymond Green.

When it comes to the Warriors, we are "witnessing a dynasty in real time..considering they defeated eight members of the NBA 75 team along the way" (McGregor, 2022).

Leaving It All on the Court

A stellar work ethic, commitment, unity of spirit, and integrity on and off the court are all the hallmarks of great athletes. Michael Jordan, Kobe Bryant, Larry Bird, Magic Johnson, Bill Russell, Wilt Chamberlain, Tim Duncan, Shaquille O'Neal, Kareem Abdul-Jabaar, and LeBron James have all left a legacy that cannot be denied. Dominating the NBA top 10 list, these men are the Greatest of All Time (GOAT).

[Mural of Kobe Bryant on the side of a building in Montreal, Canada.]

Michael Jordan, also known as "Air Jordan", was the first billionaire basketball player in NBA history. His basketball shoes were popularized in the '80s when he wore them, illegally, on the court. Regulations called for white shoes only, but Jordan insisted on promoting his red and black brand Nike Airs, even though he was fined for doing so. Nike was making millions of dollars in sales from the Jordan brand. The controversy was great for publicity, so Nike paid all of Jordan's fines, and Jordan continued wearing his shoes until the NBA relented.

Michael Jordan—astute businessman, mogul, and championship player—leaves a legacy for future generations. His athletic honors include (Sports Reference LLC, 2023):

- Hall of Fame

- 14 x All Star

- 10 x Scoring Champ

- 3 x STL Champ

- 6 x NBA Champ

- 11 x All-NBA

- 1984–85 All-Rookie

- 1984–85 Rookie of the Year

- 9 x All-Defensive

- 3 x All-Star MVP

- 1987–88 Defensive Player of the Year

- 5 x MVP

- 6 x Finals MVP

- NBA 75th Anniversary Team

- Games: 1,072

- Average points per game: 30.1

NBA Career Stats (NBA, 2023a)

- Points: 5,987

- Steals: 376

- Field goals made: 2,188

- Free throws made: 1,463

[Statue of Michael Jordan]

As a kid, LeBron James wanted to be like Mike. He couldn't afford the popular Air Jordan shoes, but he was inspired by Jordan. LeBron, also known as "King James," made history on March 6, 2019. Wearing a pair of Nikes with "thank you MJ" written on the side, James overcame Jordan as the fourth all-time leading scorer with 32,293 total career points, behind Kareem Abdul-Jabbar (38,387 points), Karl Malone (36,928 points), and Kobe Bryant (33,643 points; Beacham, 2019). His NBA stats are as follows (NBA, 2023a):

- Turnovers: 1,014

- Field goals made: 2,857

- Steals: 469

- Defensive rebounds: 2,115

- Games played: 281

- Points: 7,983

- Free throws made: 1,813

His accolades include (Sports Reference LLC, 2023):

- 19 x All-Star

- 2003–04 All-Rookie

- 2003–04 Rookie of the Year

- 2007–08 Scoring Champ

- 2019–20 AST Champ

- 4 x NBA Champ

- 19 x All-NBA

- 3 x All-Star MVP

- 6 x All-Defensive

- 4 x MVP

- 4 x Finals MVP

- NBA 75th Anniversary Team

- Career games: 1,421

- Average points per game: 27.2

- First ever *active* NBA billionaire

Small Forwards, Big Power

Small forward is a misnomer as these athletes have gigantic power. Giannis Antetokounmpo, small forward, power forward, point and shooting guard for the Milwaukee Bucks, is 7 feet tall with a wingspan of at least 7 feet 3 inches (Thompson, 2019), and weighs in at 242 pounds (Sports Reference LLC, 2023). Sporting the largest hands in the NBA, Giannis can grab the ball in midair, dunk, defend, and drive to the hole in unique and powerful ways. Nicknamed the "Greek Freak," his list of accomplishments includes (Sports Reference LLC, 2023):

- 7 x All-Star

- 2021 NBA Champion

- 6 x All-NBA

- 2013–14 All-Rookie

- 5 x All-Defensive

- 2016–17 Most Improved Player

- 2 x League MVP

- 2019–20 Defensive Player of the Year

- 2020–21 All-Star MVP

- 2021 Finals MVP

- NBA 75th Anniversary Team

2022–23 Career Summary—Giannis Antetokounmpo (Sports Reference LLC, 2023).

STATS	G	PTS	TRB	AST	FG %	FG3 %	FT %	eFG %	PER	WS
2022–23	63	31.1	11.8	5.7	55.3	27.5	64.5	5.72	29.0	8.6
Career	719	22.6	9.6	4.7	53.7	28.7	70.8	55.9	24.9	96.1

Antetokounmpo's work ethic and integrity were born out of struggle. His life is the proverbial rags to riches story. The biographical film *Rise*, streamed on Disney Plus and produced by Antetokounmpo, chronicles his family's struggles as undocumented Nigerian-Greek immigrants.

Charles and Veronica Antetokounmpo were both former athletes who had a vision for a better life for their children. Though they were both extremely hard working, they continually experienced difficulty obtaining Greek citizenship after leaving Nigeria. Keeping a roof over their children's heads was equally challenging. When Giannis and his older brother Thanasis discovered basketball, they developed a plan to learn to play well enough to help support their family. Walking 5 miles to the nearest court, and sharing a pair of shoes, they were spotted by a recruiter and hired to play for the Greek National Basketball team. Giannis was 16 years old, playing against grown men.

Giannis and Thanasis traveled together to the United States for the NBA draft. Thanasis dropped out. Their motto was, "When one family member wins, we all win." Giannis was chosen as the Milwaukee Bucks 15th pick and 15th overall in the first-round draft (Sports Reference LLC, 2023). An 18-year-old from a foreign country with no college education, he made his NBA debut on October 30, 2013. His baby face and inexperience couldn't hide his undeniable drive.

NBC Sports ranked Giannis Antetokounmpo the NBA's number one top-ranked player for the 2022–23 season. Former Los Angeles Lakers star center Shaquille "Shaq" O'Neal said of Antetokounmpo, "I denounce myself as *Superman* and I'm giving it to the Greek Freak" (Walder, 2018). Known for explosive movement, crossover craftsmanship, "freaky" speed, and the ability to effectively work both ends of the court, Giannis led the Milwaukee Bucks to their first winning season in over a decade, passing Kareem Abdul-Jabbar's all-time leading scorer record (Vincent, 2022). He led the Bucks to their first championship game in 2021, 50 years after Lew Alcindor took the team to a championship win in 1971. He was awarded the Bill Russell NBA Finals MVP award, scoring 50 points in game six against the Phoenix Suns. He tied Shaq's record with "three 40-point, 10 rebound games in a single NBA finals" (The Associated Press, 2021). As of July 21, 2021, Antetokounmpo was the only other contender to join "Michael Jordan and Hakeem Olajuwon as the only players [in] NBA history to win a regular season MVP award, a finals MVP award, and a Defensive Player of the Year award" (The Associated Press, 2021).

True to his vision of family first, Giannis sent his entire first NBA paycheck home. Not having kept anything for himself, he recognized too late that he had no money for transportation to his first game. He began running through the frosty Milwaukee streets, determined to get to the stadium 20 miles away. A Bucks fan on their way to the game saw him and gave him a ride to and from the stadium.

The middle child of five, with an infectious smile, down-to-earth attitude, intelligence, charisma, and finesse, Giannis not only accomplished what he and his brother had set out to do, he changed the trajectory of his family's life. The New York Knicks drafted Thanasis in 2014. His brother Kostas was drafted by the 76ers in 2018. Thanasis is currently on the Bucks roster with his brother: Giannis wears number 34 while Thanasis sports number 43.

Listed below are three more NBA top performers and their accomplishments (Sports Reference LLC, 2023).

Kevin Durant

- Phoenix Suns small forward, power forward

- Also known as "Durantula," "KD," "Slim Reaper"

- 13 x All-Star

- 4 x Scoring Champ

- 2 x NBA Champ

- 10 x All-NBA

- 2007–08 All-Rookie

- 2007–08 Rookie of the Year

- 2 x All-Star MVP

- 2013–14 MVP

- 2 x Finals MVP

- NBA 75th Anniversary Team

Jayson Christopher Tatum

- Small forward, power forward

- Boston Celtics 1st Round, 3rd pick/3rd overall, 2017 NBA draft

- 4 x All-Star

- 3 x All-NBA

- 2017–18 All-Rookie

- 2021–22 Eastern Conference Finals MVP

- 2022–23 All-Star MVP

Kawhi "The Klaw" Leonard
- Small forward

- Indiana Pacers 1st Round, 15th pick/15th overall, 2011 NBA draft

- 5 x All-Star

- 2014–15 STL Champ

- 2 x NBA Champ

- 5 x All-NBA

- 2011–12 All-Rookie

- 7 x All-Defensive

- 2 x Finals MVP

- 2 x Defensive Player of the Year

- 2019–20 All-Star MVP

- NBA 75th Anniversary Team

The Changing of the Guard

A point guard puts up points for the team. But how do you do that when you can't see the net clearly? You would have to ask the "Babyface Assassin," Wardell Stephen "Steph" Curry II, point guard for the Golden State Warriors, for the answer. Diagnosed in his early teens with a debilitating vision disorder called keratoconus, the NBA's top point guard could "just see the color orange really well—and usually from about 25 feet" (Villaneuva, 2022). The man who could shoot a perfect 3-pointer from 30 feet away was doing it with blurred vision.

Curry is a combination of Marlon the Magician and the Wizard of Odds. Now you see him, now you don't, or maybe you thought you saw him, and where's the ball? Swish! There's no mistaking the sound of Curry's famed all-net three-point shot from anywhere on the court, no matter how many men are guarding him. Don't be fooled by his playful antics on the gym floor, or the constant chewing on the mouth guard hanging out of the side of his mouth. "Chef Curry" serves up three-pointers like a gourmet meal. With a skip and smile, swinging his arms loosely by his sides, the 6 foot 2 inch, 185-pound "Human Torch" has a reputation for torching trash talkers and humbling his opponents with in-your-face impossible shots. Until 2019, 10 years after his NBA debut, he did so without being able to see anything but the orange ball and the basketball rim. Finally opting for contacts in 2019, his corrected vision opened up a whole new world. His athletic accolades include (Sports Reference LLC, 2023):

- 8 x All-Star

- 2015–16 Steals Champ

- 2 x League MVP

- 2021–22 All-Star MVP

- 2021–22 Finals MVP

- 2 x Scoring Champ

- 4 x NBA Champ

- 2009–10 All-Rookie

- NBA 75th Anniversary Team

- 2021–22 Western Conference Finals MVP

2022–23 Career Summary—Stephen Curry (Sports Reference LLC, 2023).

STATS	G	PTS	TRB	AST	FG %	FG3 %	FT %	eFG %	PER	WS
2022–23	56	29.4	6.1	6.3	49.3	42.7	91.5	61.4	24.1	7.8
Career	882	24.6	4.7	6.5	47.5	42.8	90.9	58.3	23.8	128.0

Steph wasn't always the name brand he is today. Born in the same hospital as LeBron James to former NBA shooting guard "Dell" Curry Senior and his wife Sonya, Steph's talent was evident from a very young age. He excelled in middle and high school but, because he was considered too small, he wasn't offered a scholarship by any of the Division I schools, even though his game was incredible. He attended Davidson College in North Carolina, a local school, scoring 28 points per game and impressing LeBron James with his style, discipline, and shooting accuracy. In 2009, still counted as a bit of an underdog and a high risk, he was chosen as the 7th draft pick for the Golden State Warriors. He exceeded every rookie expectation, with eight 30-point games in his rookie season, obtaining the rank of top 10 three-point shooters in the NBA, and finishing second as Rookie of the Year (Vincent, 2022).

A combination of outstanding marksmanship, creative artistry, resourcefulness in the paint, sheer mastery of the fadeaway, and shots that float in an almost heavenly arc to the hoop, Curry was dubbed "Threezus"—a play on the Greek God Zeus, the sky god who controls the air, including lightning and thunder. Today Curry is hailed worldwide as the greatest and most influential player of all time. An announcer in the 2015 NBA finals said, "Michael (Jordan) never shot like this or could handle the ball close to this" (Vincent, 2022). LeBron James said in an Instagram post, "You gotta guard Steph as soon as he gets out of the car. You gotta guard him when he gets out of bed in the morning." When asked on a podcast who he would like to play with on a dream team, James said, "Steph Curry." Giannis Antetokounmpo downplayed his own greatness by calling Curry "the greatest player in the world."

But Curry's accolades and achievements didn't come without costs. Chronic ankle problems that lasted off and on for 2 years had broadcasters writing him off, touting the tale that Steph shouldn't be given a contract and predicting the end of his career. In November 2012, he spent 6 months in rehab before returning to the game to challenge all the naysayers and doomsday predictors. Then began what announcers called a "3-point revolution in the NBA" (Vincent, 2022). Thunder roared from the bleachers as excited fans watched Curry and his starting teammates—Kevin Durant, Draymond Green, Klay Thompson, and JaVale McGee—wreak havoc on the Celtics including starters LeBron James, Kevin Love, J. R. Smith, George Hill, and Rodney Hood. The golden glow took over stadiums home and abroad, with the Warriors sweeping the championship 4–0.

Curry's shooting average improved tremendously after he started wearing contact lenses. By November 2022, his shooting average was 70.1%, the highest NBA shooting percentage ever. It was accurately predicted that the only person who would ever break Steph Curry's record would be Curry himself (Wirth, 2022). As of May 2023, Steph's free-throw shooting percentage is 91.5%. Improved sight meant a bigger vision.

Curry's "elite marksmanship began to challenge basketball norms" (Vincent, 2022). His masterful shooting skills, which terrorized opposing teams' defensive players, forced the developers of NBA2K to change how they designed their sports simulation video games. Curry, a man who exemplifies the love, understanding, and joy of the game, had become the cheat code, solidifying himself as the greatest shooter who ever played anywhere in the world.

Listed below are two additional NBA top performers and their accomplishments (Sports Reference LLC, 2023).

Luka Dončić

- Point and shooting guard, Dallas Mavericks

- Atlanta Hawks 1st round 3rd pick/3rd overall in 2018 NBA draft

- Nicknamed "The Matador," "The Don," "Cool Hand," "Wonder Boy"

- 4 x All-Star

- 4 x All-NBA

- 2018–19 All-Rookie

- 2018–19 Rookie of the Year

Temetrius Jamel "Ja" Morant

- Point guard

- Memphis Grizzlies 2019 NBA 1st round draft pick, 2nd pick/2nd overall

- 2 x All-Star

- 2019–20 All-Rookie

- 2019–20 Rookie of the Year

- 2021–22 Most Improved

- 2021–22 All-NBA

At the Center

Blocking shots, preventing goals in the paint, and other defensive play in the thick of things is the center's job. Nikola Jokić, also known as "The Joker," "Big Honey," and "Cookie Monster," is the center of the Denver Nuggets 2021–22 playoff team. Jokić's "special sauce" (Streeter, 2023) is temperance. He takes his time. "When he is on the court, no matter the circumstance, he seems to control time. He moves where he wants, when he wants, while every other player is slicing around the court in a frenzy" (Streeter, 2023). The 7-feet-tall center is never in a hurry. He is the most zen player in the league.

Jokić began playing professional basketball at 17 years old in his native Serbia. Even then, he was never rushed. He was always a thoughtful player, scoping out the territory before moving in on his prey.

Jokić was drafted by the Denver Nuggets in 2014 as the 11th pick in the second round. His talent is the ability to think three and four steps ahead, to see prophetically before things happen, strategize the next best move, and act accordingly. Greg Applebaum, director of the Human Performance Optimization Lab at U.C. San Diego, studies athletes' cognition. He said of Jokić, "The way he tracks information around him, knowing where everybody is on the court, making perfectly timed passes all the time to open teammates, takes a special mental ability" (Streeter, 2023). Jokić, like a human computer, can calculate and time the best possible move for the moment. He led the Denver Nuggets to their first NBA Finals championship win over the Los Angeles Lakers in a 4–0 sweep. Other accolades include (Sports Reference LLC, 2023):

- 5 x All-Star

- 5 x All-NBA

- 2015–16 All-Rookie

- 2 x MVP

2022–23 Career Summary—Nikola Jokić (Sports Reference LLC, 2023).

STATS	G	PTS	TRB	AST	FG %	FG3 %	FT %	eFG %	PER	WS
2022–23	69	24.5	11.5	9.8	63.2	38.3	82.2	66.0	31.5	14.9
Career	596	20.2	10.5	6.6	55.3	34.8	82.9	58.9	27.7	94.5

Another superstar center is Joel Embiid of the Philadelphia 76ers. Embiid, also known as "The Process," originally hails from Yaounde, Cameroon. His athletic accolades include (Sports Reference LLC, 2023):

- 2014 NBA 3rd overall first-round draft pick

- 6 x All-Star

- 2 x Scoring Champ

- 5 x All-NBA

- 2016–17 All-Rookie

- 3 x All-Defensive

- 2022–23 MVP

Game Time

How to Play

Divide your group into teams or play one-on-one with a friend. Answer all the *Game Time* questions from the text or your knowledge of basketball for two points each. Test your basketball trivia expertise by answering the bonus questions for three points each. Tally up your score at the end of this chapter and all the previous chapters to find out who wins the championship.

1. Which team is the top reigning dynasty in 2022–23?

   a. Los Angeles Lakers

   b. Milwaukee Bucks

   c. Golden State Warriors

2. What is the last name of the three brothers who all won NBA championship rings in the same year?

   a. Antetokounmpo

   b. Curry

   c. Ball

3. Which team created an unstoppable dynasty from 1990–98?

   a. Bulls

   b. Celtics

   c. Lakers

4. What is the name of the film about Giannis Antetokounmpo's life?

    a. *Above the Rim*

    b. *Glory Road*

    c. *Rise*

5. Who beat Reggie Miller's three-point shooting record?

    a. Ray Allen

    b. LeBron James

    c. Kevin Durant

6. Who was considered the NBA's greatest long range shooter with 2,560 three-point baskets?

    a. Reggie Miller

    b. Julius Erving

    c. Ray Allen

7. Where did Steph Curry break Ray Allen's record?

    a. Madison Square Garden

    b. Chase Center

    c. Gainbridge Fieldhouse

8. When did Stephen Curry surpass Ray Allen's three-point shooting record?

    a. 2021

    b. 2019

c. 2022

d. 2020

BONUS

1. Which NBA MVP served in the military in his off season?

    a. Giannis

    b. LeBron

    c. Hakeem Olajuwon

2. Which basketball movie is about the Chicago Bulls?

    a. *The Last Dance*

    b. *The Last Chance*

    c. *The Way Back*

3. Which NBA G.O.A.T. stars in the basketball movie *Space Jam—A New Legacy*?

    a. Allen Iverson

    b. Michael Jordan

    c. LeBron James

4. What was the reason Michael Jordan's shoe was banned by the NBA?

    a. The shoes did not follow the uniform regulations.

    b. Only certain brands were allowed in the NBA.

    c. The shoes were not comfortable for most players.

Conclusion

Naismith's basketball game, originally designed to keep his bored students busy, has become one of the greatest sports the world over. It has survived the many tests of time. Children as young as 5 and adults in their 70s are still playing it.

The NCAA, which began with one college team playing at YMCAs, is now a billion-dollar machine. In 2022, data showed that "women basketball players are the second highest paid college athletes" (Freeman, 2022). This is largely due to a 2021 United States Supreme Court ruling that gave college athletes the right to use their name and image to promote products and services. Zia Cooke, the highest paid college athlete, makes about $8,000 every time she endorses a product to her 228,000 Instagram followers (Freeman, 2022). Not only is she ranked among the top athletes in the NCAA, she is also a top earner.

Slow games, metal cages, and media disinterest are no longer the hallmark of professional basketball. Games are now streamed and televised globally. Professional players earn high six- and seven-figure salaries whether they are on the bench or on the court. Many young players come into six-figure deals straight out of high school or college. Basketball players like LeBron James and Michael Jordan have become billionaire businessmen with endorsement deals, investments, and other smart money moves.

Gambling is now part and parcel of league revenue. Fans can create fantasy teams made up of fan favorites, or join a fantasy league on popular fantasy sports sites like FanDuel and DraftKings, and earn points based on the actual players' performances. It is still illegal, however, for real teams to bet on one another.

Dynasties and legacies are still being made as the old guard makes way for the new. The Naismith Memorial Basketball Hall of Fame is located in Springfield, Massachusetts, where it all began. The museum houses a complete history of basketball. The Hall of Fame honors those who have gone before, those currently existing and retired, and the up and coming generations of all-time greats including coaches, referees, and athletes. From a peach basket and a soccer ball, one man made history.

Game Time Answer Guide

Game Time—Chapter 1 Answers

1. C

2. C

3. D

4. B

5. B

BONUS

1. D

2. A

3. C

4. C

Game Time—Chapter 2 Answers

1. B

2. B

3. True

4. True

5. Pistons

6. C

7. A

8. A

9. B

10. A

11. B

12. False

Game Time—Chapter 3 Answers

1. B

2. A

3. B

4. C

5. C

BONUS

1. C

2. A

Game Time—Chapter 4 Answers

1. B

2. C + D

3. D

4. D

5. C

6. B

BONUS
1. One
2. B

Game Time—Chapter 5 Answers

1. B

2. D

3. B

4. C

5. C

BONUS

1. A

2. A

3. C

Game Time—Chapter 6 Answers

1. B

2. C

3. A

4. A

5. C

BONUS

1. A

2. B

3. C

4. A

5. C

Game Time—Chapter 7 Answers

1. C

2. A

3. A

4. C

5. A

6. A

7. A

8. A

BONUS

1. A

2. C

3. C

4. A

References

Aschburner, S. (2022, March 31). *How a trio of pioneers gave rise to racial integration in the NBA.* NBA. https://www.nba.com/news/how-chuck-cooper-nat-clifton-earl-lloyd-changed-nba-racial-integration

The Associated Press. (2021, July 20). *Giannis Antetokounmpo wins the 2021 Bill Russell NBA Finals MVP award.* NBA. https://www.nba.com/news/giannis-wins-2021-finals-mvp

Basketball.org. (n.d.). *A brief history of basketball.* Basketball. https://www.basketball.org/history/index/

Beacham, G. (2019). *LeBron passes Jordan for 4th in career scoring.* NBA. https://www.nba.com/news/lebron-james-passes-michael-jordan-nba-career-scoring-list

Biography.com Editors. (2020, November 17). *Kevin Durant. NBA All-Star Kevin Durant nabbed several scoring titles with the Oklahoma City Thunder before winning back-to-back championships with Golden State Warriors.* Biography. https://www.biography.com/athletes/kevin-durant

Dougherty, J. (2020, June 30). *The tragic death of 7-Foot-7 NBA legend Manute Bol.* Sportscasting. https://www.sportscasting.com/the-tragic-death-of-7-foot-7-nba-legend-manute-bol/

Eluemuno, C. (2022, November 8). *5 NBA superteams that failed due to lack of chemistry.* Sportskeeda. https://www.sportskeeda.com/basketball/5-nba-superteams-failed-due-lack-chemistry

Espinoza, A. (2023, May 1). *Draymond Green reveals Steph Curry delivered epic speech before Game 7 vs. Kings.* MSN. https://www.msn.com/en-us/sports/nba/draymon-green-reveals-steph-curry-delivered-epic-speech-before-game-7-vs-kings/ar-AA1azEWb

ESPN.com. (2021, October 21). *NBA75: Meet the best players in league history.* ESPN. https://www.espn.com/nba/story/_/id/32432119/nba-75-greatest-players-all-complete-list

Freeman, A. (2022, April 17). *Zia Cooke, one of the highest paid college basketball players, talks about impact of sponsorship deals.* CBS News.https://www.cbsnews.com/news/zia-cooke-university-of-south-carolina-womens-basketball-sponsorship-deals/

Gay, C. (2021, February 1). *The Black Fives: A history of the era that led to the NBA's racial integration.* The Sporting News. https://www.sportingnews.com/ca/nba/news/the-black-fives-a-history-of-the-era-that-led-to-the-nbas-racial-integration/8fennuvt00hl1odmregcrbbtj

Gildea, D. (2011, August 21). *Sherman White, basketball star that few knew, dies at 82.* Masslive. https://www.masslive.com/sports/2011/08/basketball_ball_star_that_few.html

Goalcast. (2022, March 4). *Why did the NBA fear this 5'3 basketball player? | Muggsy Bogues | Goalcast.* [Video]. https://www.youtube.com/watch?v=h-XqjEapYpY

Golden State Warriors. (2021, December 14). *Warriors Ground: Stephen Curry's golden record.* [Video]. https://www.youtube.com/watch?v=Icsa6yt_DXo&t=118s

Grove, R. (2021, May 5). *How the Harlem Globetrotters rose from midwest obscurity to become global stars: Photos.* History. https://www.history.com/news/harlem-globetrotters-photos

Harlem World Magazine. (2019, September 4). *Bob Douglas, father of black professional basketball and founder of the NY Rens basketball team.* Harlem World Magazine. https://www.harlemworldmagazine.com/bob-douglas-father-of-black-professional-basketball-and-founder-of-the-ny-rens-basketball-team/

Hermann, A. (2022, February 28). *The first college basketball game on TV was Pitt vs. Fordham in 1940.* NCAA. https://www.ncaa.com/news/basketball-men/article/2022-02-28/first-televised-college-basketball-game-featured-pitt-and-fordham-february-1940

History.com Editors. (2020, July 30). *The NBA is born.* History. https://www.history.com/this-day-in-history/nba-is-born

The HistoryMakers. (2019). *Earl Francis Lloyd's Biography.* The HistoryMakers. https://www.thehistorymakers.org/biography/earl-francis-lloyd-41

Horsting, L. (2019, April 3). *Steph Curry opens up about vision problems.* Warriors Wire. https://warriorswire.usatoday.com/2019/04/03/steph-curry-the-nbas-greatest-shooter-ever-has-had-vision-problems-his-whole-career/

Imaz A. (2011, September 28). *10 greatest NBA teams of all time.* Bleacher Report. https://bleacherreport.com/articles/865311-10-greatest-nba-teams-of-all-time

Klein, C. (2022, August 15). *How a Canadian invented basketball.* History. https://www.history.com/news/how-a-canadian-invented-basketball

Li, D. K. (2019, September 27). *NBA to start measuring exact height of players.* NBC News. https://www.nbcnews.com/news/us-news/nba-teams-will-start-measuring-height-their-players-real-n1059631

Litsky, F. (1998, September 18). *Junius Kellogg is dead at 71; Refused bribe in 50's scandal.* The New York Times. https://www.nytimes.com/1998/09/18/sports/junius-kellogg-is-dead-at-71-refused-bribe-in-50-s-scandal.html

Logan, R. G., Mokray, W. G., Donald, L. W., & The Editors of Encyclopedia Britannica. (2020). *Basketball | Definition, History, Rules, Players, & Facts.* Britannica. https://www.britannica.com/sports/basketball#ref29665

LQG. (2016, June 15). *The 10 dirtiest players in NBA history!* [Video]. https://www.youtube.com/watch?v=8iVo7rsLJRA&t=3s

Luke. (2021, November 1). *Top 5 longest shots in NBA history (with videos).* Dunk or Three. https://dunkorthree.com/longest-shot-in-nba-history

Luke. (2023). *Dunk or Three: Help you play better basketball.* Dunk or Three. https://dunkorthree.com/

Majidi, M. (2023, January 5). *TV advertising revenue during March Madness 2019.* Statista. https://www.statista.com/statistics/219961/tv-advertising-revenue-during-march-madness/

McGregor, G. (2022, June 15). *Where do the Warriors rank among all-time NBA dynasties? How run compares to Lakers, Bulls, Celtics and others.* The Sporting News.

https://www.sportingnews.com/us/nba/news/warriors-celtics-lakers-bulls-dynasties-rank/u3d48ub5ldkrp3p9kzc7vkgs#Boston%20Celtics

McMahon, C. (2021, October 30). *The Birth of the Bag: 75 Years of NBA Salaries*. Boardroom. https://boardroom.tv/nba-player-salary-history/

MDJ. (2019). *Basketball Before the NBA (1891-1950): A Brief History.* [Video] https://www.youtube.com/watch?v=a-ecd9-HEq0

Morris, B. (2014, April 15). *Just how bad were the "Bad Boys"?* FiveThirtyEight. https://fivethirtyeight.com/features/just-how-bad-were-the-bad-boys/

National Basketball Association. (2023). *Teams | Stats*. NBA. https://www.nba.com/stats/teams

NBA. (2023a). *All Time Leaders | Stats.|* NBA. https://www.nba.com/stats/alltime

NBA. (2023b, April 15). *#6 WARRIORS at #3 KINGS | FULL GAME 1 HIGHLIGHTS | April 15, 2023.* [Video]. https://www.youtube.com/watch?v=dXMVjUnip-Q

NCAA. (2022). *Finances.* NCAA. https://www.ncaa.org/sports/2021/5/4/finances.aspx

Nonstop. (2020, March 14). *Other short nba players who made their mark.* Bing. https://www.bing.com/videos/search?q=other+short+nba+players+who+made+their+mark&docid

Pro Basketball Encyclopedia. (2023). *John Wendelken.* Pro Basketball Encyclopedia.

https://probasketballencyclopedia.com/player/John-Wendelken/

Raje, A. (2023, April 11). *Who are the 5 most dominant NBA teams in history?* Sportskeeda. https://www.sportskeeda.com/basketball/who-5-dominant-nba-teams-history#

Sah, S. (2023, February 27). *Top 10 best NBA players of all time [2022 Update].* Players Bio. https://playersbio.com/best-nba-player/

SI Staff. (1991, November 11). *Sports Illustrated Vault.* https://vault.si.com/

Sports Reference LLC. (2023, May 6). *Giannis Antetokounmpo Stats.* Basketball Reference. https://www.basketball-reference.com/players/a/antetgi01.html

Springfield College. (2015, December 18). *PBS's NewsHour with Judy Woodruff highlights Naismith audio and Springfield College.* [Video]. https://www.youtube.com/watch?v=JlgYkCctZcM

Streeter, K. (2023, May 22). *Nikola Jokic has mastered the art of slowness.* The New York Times. https://www.nytimes.com/2023/05/22/sports/basketball/nikoa-jokic-denver-nuggets-game-4.html

Thompson, D. (2019, February 26). *What Are the Wingspan and Vertical of NBA Star Giannis Antetokounmpo?* Sportscasting. https://www.sportscasting.com/wingspan-and-vertical-giannis-antetokounmpo/

Villaneuva, V. (2022, January 11). *Stephen Curry on shooting mastery despite poor eyesight.* Basketball Network. https://www.basketballnetwork.net/latest-news/stephen-curry-on-shooting-mastery

Vincent, J. (2022, December 2). *Giannis Antetokounmpo—The Greek Freak (Original Career Documentary).* [Video]. https://www.youtube.com/watch?v=x0jzUPN27tw

Walder, C. (2018, November 30). *Shaq bestows the "Superman" nickname upon Antetokounmpo.* The Score. https://www.thescore.com/nba/news/1666302

Whistle. (2013, October 6). *Muggsy Bogues At The Basketball Hall Of Fame.* [Video]. https://www.youtube.com/watch?v=-Y86_vw5iFY&t=78s

Wikipedia Contributors. (2020, January 17). *Chuck Cooper (basketball).* Wikipedia. https://en.wikipedia.org/wiki/Chuck_Cooper_(basketball)

Wirth, T. (2022, November 17). *Steph on pace to shatter historic 2018 true shooting record.* Sports. https://www.nbcsports.com/bayarea/warriors/steph-curry-pace-shatter-true-shooting-record-huge-2022-23-season

Worthington, T. (2020, August 8). *Top 10 NBA teams of all-time.* Lineups. https://www.lineups.com/articles/top-10-nba-teams-of-all-time/

Wronged Sports. (2019, October 24). *Wronged sports Ep 5: New York City gambling scandal.* [Video]. https://www.youtube.com/watch?v=Tek8D1XatUs

YounGala. (2021, May 4). *NBA legends And players explain how special Muggsy Bogues was.* [Video]. https://www.youtube.com/watch?v=3VtdVPrjAIE

Photo Credits

Bennett, D. (2020). *Kobe Bryant* [Image]. Unsplash. https://unsplash.com/photos/nFjLHE4vmn4

Castillo, R. (2022, October 15). *Championship trophy [Image]*. Unsplash. https://unsplash.com/photos/qZJBLmz2lI4

DeYoung, B. (2021). *Television* [Image]. Unsplash. https://unsplash.com/photos/tJzJXbO-pbs

Dragotta, T. (2018). *Spalding basketball* [Image]. Unsplash. https://unsplash.com/photos/mu7amBMAT3E

Florida Memory. (2023, April 28). *FSU basketball player* [Image]. Unsplash. https://unsplash.com/photos/CfZDZSZO-lY

Haupt, M. (2022). *Golden State Warriors cap* [Image]. Unsplash. https://unsplash.com/photos/dQXGnaK8A9E

Lee, F. (2021, May 9). *Michael Jordan statue* [Image]. Unsplash. https://unsplash.com/photos/PFzZimTsxlE

National Library of Scotland. (2023, May 7). *Scottish military men and women playing basketball* [Image]. Unsplash. https://unsplash.com/photos/ZvqR9s2B1tw

The New York Public Library. (2019). *Old basketball* [Image]. Unsplash. https://unsplash.com/photos/mcXlRX_9sd0

Picchiottino, D. (2022, August 31). *New York Stadium* [Image]. Unsplash. https://unsplash.com/photos/w_LBxBvafMM

Pixabay. (2008). Kings versus Houston [Image]. Pexels. https://www.pexels.com/photo/arena-athlete-ball-basketball-163423/

Rice, J. (2022). *March Madness* [Image]. Unsplash. https://unsplash.com/photos/mS-VWgfUHbQ

Ryan. (2018). *Basketball stadium* [Image]. Unsplash. https://unsplash.com/photos/OywyPkrDEvg

Weaver, L. (2020). *College player* [Image]. Unsplash. https://unsplash.com/photos/M5YKACTmdpo

Winegeart, K. (2020, September 18). *LeBron James* [Image]. Unsplash. https://unsplash.com/photos/CGmzhaiPRjs